About the Author

I0004845

Mr. Sagar Salunke has 11 years of experience in automation testing using Selenium Webdriver. He has worked on large investment banking projects in tier-1 Software Companies in UK, USA and Europe

He has designed automation frameworks in Selenium with Ruby that is widely used in the IT industry.

His hobbies include travelling and watching football.

Who is this book for

This book is for software testing professionals who want to test the web applications by automation testing using selenium webdriver. All examples in this book are given in Ruby. So it will be good for the reader to have the Ruby background. This book covers all basic as well as advanced concepts in Selenium Webdriver in Ruby.

What is covered in this book

This book covers below topics on Selenium Webdriver.

1. Background of Selenium Webdriver and Automation testing.
2. Installation of Selenium in Ruby in windows.
3. Identification of web elements using xpath, css, id, class name, tag name, link text, partial link text and using name attribute.
4. Manipulating common web controls like editboxes, comboboxes and checkboxes with selenium in Ruby.
5. Automating complex keyboard and mouse Interactions using Actions class.
6. Practical challenges and Solutions (Nested Tables, Text based elements identification, Ajax, JavascriptExecutor, Advanced CSS and Xpath, DOM Methods).
7. Synchronization methods in Selenium Webdriver.
8. Working with multiple windows, alerts and frames.
9. Handling Selenium Webdriver Exceptions.
10. Ruby Basics + Taking Screenshots in Selenium Webdriver.
11. Selenium Tools and features like Selenium IDE, Grid and Desired Capabilities.
12. Different frameworks like Keyword driven automation frameworks, Data driven frameworks.

Table of Contents

1. SELENIUM Basics

> *In this chapter you will get familiar with selenium Webdriver. You will also learn about the Installation of Jdk and Eclipse along with Selenium Webdriver. We will also write a simple Ruby program in Eclipse*

1.1 What is Selenium?

Selenium is an open source web application testing framework released under apache license. Selenium can be installed on all platforms like

1. Windows.
2. Linux.
3. Macintosh.

It supports programming in many languages as mentioned below.

1. Java
2. .Net
3. Ruby
4. Python
5. PHP
6. Perl
7. JavaScript

1.2 What is selenium Webdriver?

Selenium Webdriver is the successor to Selenium RC. In earlier versions of selenium we needed Selenium RC server to execute the test scripts.

Now we can use Webdriver to execute the test on particular browser. For each browser we have a separate web driver which accepts the selenium commands and drives the browser under test.

1.3 Browsers supported by Selenium.

Below is the list of browsers supported by the selenium Webdriver.

1. Internet Explorer
2. Google Chrome
3. Firefox
4. Opera
5. Safari

Please note that for each browser, there is a separate web driver implementation.

1.4 Choosing technology for selenium.

As mentioned earlier, there are lot of languages that can be used for selenium scripting. Choosing the language depends upon the below factors.

1. Skill Set of employees in the organisation.
2. Training required on specific language.

I have selected Ruby as a programming language for selenium scripting. So in this book you will see all examples in Ruby only. But the same logic applies to other languages with some syntactical differences.

1.5 Installing selenium with Ruby.

Well – Now let us understand the installation steps in selenium.

The list of Softwares you will need is given below.

1. Download and install Ruby Installer from the URL http://rubyinstaller.org/downloads/
2. Install selenium webdriver using command **gem install selenium-webdriver**
3. Execute the ruby code using command **ruby selenium_code.rb**

After installing ruby, edit the PATH environment variable to include the path of the folder where you installed the ruby.

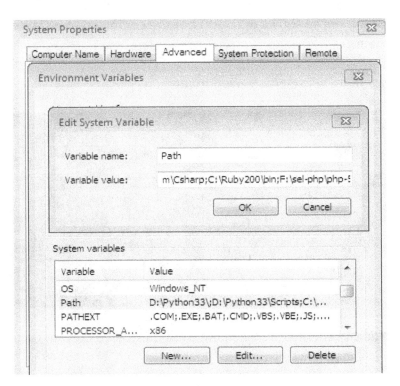

I installed the ruby at c:\Ruby200\. So I edited the PATH variable to include the path c:\Ruby200\Bin.
To check if the ruby is installed properly, run below command in the command prompt.
>ruby –v
If you see the version of the ruby in the output, it means that ruby is installed properly.

```
C:\Windows\system32\cmd.exe

C:\Users\sagar>ruby -v
ruby 2.0.0p481 (2014-05-08) [i386-mingw32]

C:\Users\sagar>
```

Next you need to install the selenium webdriver Gem. Below image shows the output of the command to install Gem.

>gem install selenium-webdriver

```
C:\Users\sagar>gem install selenium-webdriver
Successfully installed selenium-webdriver-2.42.0
Parsing documentation for selenium-webdriver-2.42.0
unable to convert "\xE0" from ASCII-8BIT to UTF-8 for li
efox/native/linux/amd64/x_ignore_nofocus.so, skipping
unable to convert "\xB0" from ASCII-8BIT to UTF-8 for li
efox/native/linux/x86/x_ignore_nofocus.so, skipping
unable to convert "\xD0" from ASCII-8BIT to UTF-8 for li
ari/resources/SafariDriver.safariextz, skipping
WARNING:  Unable to pull data from 'https://rubygems.org
//rubygems.org/specs.4.8.gz)
WARNING:  Unable to pull data from 'https://rubygems.org
//rubygems.org/specs.4.8.gz)
WARNING:  Unable to pull data from 'https://rubygems.org
//rubygems.org/specs.4.8.gz)
WARNING:  Unable to pull data from 'https://rubygems.org
//rubygems.org/specs.4.8.gz)
1 gem installed
```

You can check if the Selenium Gem is installed on your local machine by below command.

>gem list --local

You will see all the gems installed on your machine after executing above command. It also shows the version of the gem installed.

In below image, third last gem is the one we have just installed –> selenium-webdriver(2.42.0)

```
C:\Windows\system32\cmd.exe

*** REMOTE GEMS ***


C:\Users\sagar>gem list --local

*** LOCAL GEMS ***

bigdecimal (1.2.0)
childprocess (0.5.3)
ffi (1.9.3 x86-mingw32)
io-console (0.4.2)
json (1.7.7)
minitest (4.3.2)
multi_json (1.10.1)
psych (2.0.0)
rake (0.9.6)
rdoc (4.0.0)
rubyzip (1.1.6)
selenium-webdriver (2.42.0)
test-unit (2.0.0.0)
websocket (1.0.7)
```

So far the installation of Ruby and Selenium Gem is done successfully. Now we can start writing the automation scripts in Ruby. In next chapter, we will write simple ruby script to automate the browsers like chrome, firefox, IE, safari, opera etc.

2. First Script in Selenium Webdriver

> *In this chapter, you will learn how to inspect the web elements in different browsers like IE, Firefox, and Google Chrome etc. You will also learn how to write a simple selenium script in Ruby.*

Before I jump to first script in selenium webdriver, let me explain you how you can use developer tools provided by browsers like IE, chrome, Firefox while automating the web applications.

Inspecting Elements in Google Chrome.

Google chrome provides very nice tool to inspect the elements on the webpage. You have to just right click on the web element and then select last menu item from the context menu – Inspect. After you click on it, you will see the source code of that element as displayed in below image.

When you take your mouse over the html source code, corresponding element on the web page is also highlighted. This helps us to know all the values of the attributes of the element.

In next figure, we have inspected the editbox called full name at the URL
http://register.rediff.com/register/register.php

The corresponding html source code is

```
<input type="text" onblur="fieldTrack(this);"
name="name" value="" style="width:185px;"
maxlength="61">
```

So for the full name editbox, we have below attributes and values.

1. type = text
2. onblur=fieldTrack(this);
3. name=name
4. value=
5. style=width:185px;
6. maxlength=61

You can use this information to write css expressions and xpath expressions which are used to identify the elements on the webpage.

Create a Rediffmail account

Full Name   :

Choose a Rediffmail ID   :

Password   :

Retype password   :

Alternate Email Address   :

| Undo |
| Redo |
| Cut |
| Copy |
| Paste |
| Paste as plain text |
| Delete |
| Spell-checker options |
| Select all |
| Inspect element |

s Network Sources Timeline Profiles Resources
<table cellspacing="0" cellpadding="0" bo
eight="54" align="center" class="f14">
▼<tbody>
  ▶<tr>…</tr>
  ▶<tr>…</tr>
  ▼<tr>
    <td width="180">Full Name</td>

Figure 0-1 - Inspecting Elements in Chrome

Inspecting Elements in Internet Explorer.

Internet Explorer 10 and higher provides the developer tools from where you can inspect the elements on the webpage. You have to click on the arrow (circled in the red) and then click on the element on the webpage as displayed in below image.

13

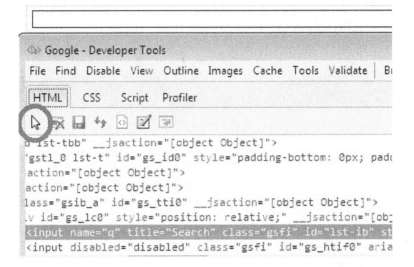

Figure 0-2 - Inspecting Elements in IE

Inspecting Elements in Firefox.

Inspecting elements in Firefox is similar to chrome. Inspecting elements will help you knowing the attributes of the elements like name, id etc. which in turn can be used in selenium scripts.

Figure 0-3 - Inspecting element in Firefox

Let us start with scripting right away. Have a look at below example.

2.1 Sample Selenium Program

```
#include the webdriver gem
require "selenium-webdriver"

#launch firefox
driver = Selenium::WebDriver.for
:firefox

#set the implicit wait timeout for
3 seconds
```

```
driver.manage.timeouts.implicit_wai
t = 3

#navigate to website
driver.navigate.to
"http://selenium-interview-
questions.blogspot.in/2014/03/selen
ium-webdriver-test-page.html"

#Maximize the window.
driver.manage.window.maximize

#quit the driver.
driver.quit
```

Save above script in abc.rb file

2.2 How to execute ruby script.

Open command prompt and use below command.

```
> Ruby f:\sel-ruby\abc.rb
```

Above command will launch the firefox browser and then close it.

You can also execute above script by just double clicking on the file. But before that you will have to associate .rb extension to the Ruby.exe application using below steps.
1. Right click on the ruby script file
2. Select open with...menu and then select choose default program

3. In next window, browse to the ruby installation directory and select ruby.exe file in bin folder.
4. Click on ok.

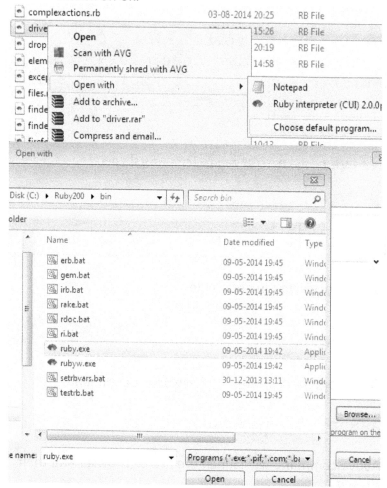

Once you follow above steps, you will be able to execute the script by just double clicking on it.

2.3 Explanation

In above program, We have included the selenium-webdriver library in first statement. Then we have created the new instance of Web Driver for Firefox. In the next statements we have set the default object synchronization timeout (3 seconds). Then we have used navigate method to open http://selenium-interview-questions.blogspot.in/2014/03/selenium-webdriver-test-page.html webpage.

At the end we have closed the browser. Please note that creating a webdriver for other browsers like internet explorer, chrome and opera is also similar. You just need to change the second line in above program as shown in below script.

```
#launch chrome
driver = Selenium::WebDriver.for
:chrome

#launch Internet Explorer
driver = Selenium::WebDriver.for
:ie

#launch safari
driver = Selenium::WebDriver.for
:safari

#launch opera
driver = Selenium::WebDriver.for
:opera
```

Please note that all browsers must be already installed in your system before you execute above scripts.

I did not have safari installed on my system. So when I tried to launch the safari, it threw below exception.

```
 C:\Ruby200\bin\ruby.exe
No such file or directory - Safari data directory not found
pData\Roaming/Apple Computer/Safari
["C:/Ruby200/lib/ruby/gems/2.0.0/gems/selenium-webdriver-2.
driver/safari/extensions.rb:126:in `install_directory'", "C
ms/2.0.0/gems/selenium-webdriver-2.42.0/lib/selenium/webdri
.rb:61:in `install'", "C:/Ruby200/lib/ruby/gems/2.0.0/gems/
42.0/lib/selenium/webdriver/safari/bridge.rb:16:in `initial
b/ruby/gems/2.0.0/gems/selenium-webdriver-2.42.0/lib/seleni
river.rb:47:in `new'", "C:/Ruby200/lib/ruby/gems/2.0.0/gems
.42.0/lib/selenium/webdriver/common/driver.rb:47:in `for'",
/gems/2.0.0/gems/selenium-webdriver-2.42.0/lib/selenium/web
", "F:/sel-ruby/basic.rb:3:in `<main>'"]
```

When working with Selenium Webdriver and Internet Explorer, ensure that protected mode is enabled for all zones as displayed in below figure.

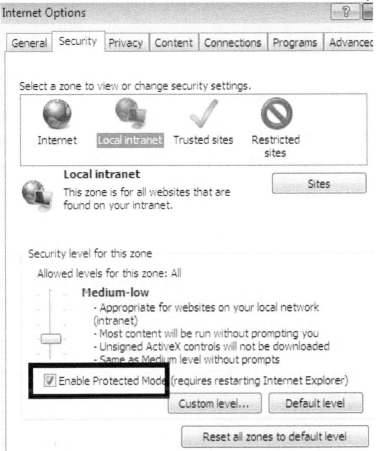

Figure 0-4 - Enable protected mode for all Zones

You must know important classes and interfaces provided by selenium webdriver API in Ruby. Here is the list of important classes in selenium webdriver API in Ruby.

1. Selenium::WebDriver::Driver
2. Selenium::WebDriver::Element
3. Selenium::WebDriver::Navigation
4. Selenium::WebDriver::Options
5. Selenium::WebDriver::TargetLocator
6. Selenium::WebDriver::Timeouts

3. Element identification methods in SELENIUM

In this chapter, you will learn about different methods of element identification in selenium webdriver like xpath, css, id, name, class_name, tag_name, link_text, partial_link_text. You will also come to know the difference between find_element and find_elements methods.

As illustrated in the first program, It is very simple to create the webdriver instance and navigate to the webpage. In testing web application we need to perform operations on the webpage like clicking on the link or button, selecting the checkbox or radio button, choosing an item from the dropdown etc.

In selenium terminology, all objects in webpage are treated as webelements. So it is very important to identify the elements first and then perform some operations on them. Selenium provides plenty of methods to identify the web elements as mentioned below.

1. Xpath
2. CSS
3. Id
4. Name
5. Class Name
6. Tag Name

7. Link Text
8. Partial Link Text

We are going to look into each of these methods one by one.

3.1 Xpath

Xpath is the web technology/standard that is used to access elements from the webpage or xml document. Detailed discussion of the xpath is beyond the scope of this book. We will see just simple examples to give you the idea of xpath. You can learn the basics of xpath at http://www.w3schools.com/xpath/xpath_syntax.asp

Examples – Suppose you want to identify the link of which href attribute contains Google.

Xpath expression for above example - //a[contains(@href,'google')]

Below code will find the first link of which **href** attribute contains google

element = driver.find_element(:xpath, '//a[contains(@href, "google")]')

Below table gives some sample xpath expressions.

Find all elements with tag input	`//input`
Find all input tag element having attribute type = 'hidden'	`//input[@type='hidden']`

Find all input tag element having attribute type = 'hidden' and name attribute = 'ren'	`//input[@type='hidden'][@name='ren']`
Find all input tag element with attribute type containing 'hid'	`//input[contains(@type,'hid')]`
Find all input tag element with attribute type starting with 'hid'	`//input[starts-with(@type,'hid')]`
Find all elements having innertext = 'password'	`//*[text()='Password']`
Find all td elements having innertext = 'password'	`//td[text()='Password']`
Find all next siblings of td tag having innertext = 'gender'	`//td[text()='Gender']//following-sibling::*`
Find all elements in the 2nd next sibling of td tag having innertext = 'gender'	`//td[text()='Gender']//following-sibling::*[2]//*`
Find input elements in the 2nd next sibling of td tag having innertext = 'gender'	`//td[text()='Gender']//following-sibling::*[2]//input`
Find the td which contains font element containing the text '12'	`//td[font[contains(text(),'12')]]`
Find all the preceding siblings of the td which contains font element containing the text '12'	`//td[font[contains(text(),'12')]]//preceding-sibling::*`

Below example illustrates how we can use xpath in selenium webdriver using Ruby. The xpath expression that we have used is -

```
//input[starts-with(@onblur,'field')]
```

Above xpath expression will identify the element with tag name as input and of which onblur attribute's value starts with **field**.

```ruby
require "selenium-webdriver"
begin
driver = Selenium::WebDriver.for
:chrome
driver.navigate.to
"http://selenium-interview-
questions.blogspot.in/2014/03/selen
ium-webdriver-test-page.html"

element =
driver.find_element(:xpath,
'//table[@id="empdata"]')

#puts
element.find_element(:tag_name,'td'
).text

tdtags=element.find_elements(:tag_n
ame,'td')

tdtags.each do |td|
      puts td.text
end


#element.send_keys "Ruby"
```

```ruby
puts driver.title

#catch exceptions if any
rescue Exception => e
  puts e.message
  puts e.backtrace.inspect
end

temp = gets.chomp

driver.quit
```

You can also use below tools to learn xpath
1. Xpath Checker
2. Firebug.

In Google chrome, you can copy the xpath of any element very easily. Below figure shows how we can do it.

Figure 0-1 - Copy xpath and CSS path in Chrome

In other browsers like IE and FF also, you will find similar options in developer tools.

You can also use console window to try and test xpath and CSS expressions from the console window provided in chrome.

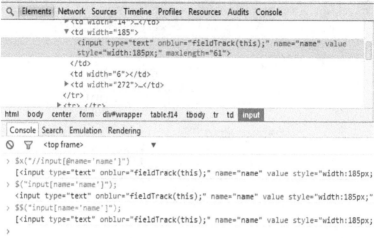

Figure 0-2 - Console window in chrome

To test xpath expressions, you can use below syntax.
`$x("//input[@name='name']")`

To test CSS expressions, you can use below syntax. $ will return only first matched element.
`$("input[name='name']")`

To test CSS expressions, you can use below syntax. $$ will return all matched elements.
`$$("input[name='name']")`

3.2 CSS

CSS selectors can also be used to find the web elements in a web page. Css selectors are always preferred over xpath expressions as it is faster and standard across all browsers.

You can visit

http://www.w3schools.com/cssref/css_selectors.asp to learn about css selectors.

```
element = driver.find_element(:css,
'table[id="empdata"]')

element = driver.find_element(:css,
'#empdata')
```

Above code will identify the first element having id equal to empdata.

Below table shows commonly used css Selectors in Selenium.

Find all elements with tag input	`input`
Find all input tag element having attribute type = 'hidden'	`input[type='hidden']`
Find all input tag element having attribute type = 'hidden' and name attribute = 'ren'	`input[type='hidden'][name='ren']`
Find all input tag element with attribute type containing 'hid'	`input[type*='hid']`
Find all input tag element with attribute type starting with 'hid'	`input[type^='hid']`
Find all input tag element with attribute type ending with 'den'	`input[type$='den']`

Below example demonstrates how we can use cssSelectors to identify the elements in Ruby.

3.3 Id

This method can be used to identify any object in the web page. Only requirement is that the object should have an id attribute associated with it.

Example – Suppose you want to click on the button having id as "empdata". You can use below syntax to click on the button.

```
element = driver.find_element(:id,
'empdata')
element.click
```

3.4 Name

This method can be used to identify any object in the web page.

Only requirement is that the object should have a name attribute associated with it.

Example – Suppose you want to click on the button with name "register". You can use below syntax to click on the button.

```
element =
driver.find_element(:name,
'register')
element.click
```

3.5 Class Name

This method can be used to identify any object in the web page. Only requirement is that the object should have a class attribute associated with it.

Example – Suppose you want to click on the button having class as "c1". You can use below syntax to click on the button.

```
element =
driver.find_element(:class_name,
'c1')
```

3.6 Tag Name

This method can be used to identify any element in the web page with given tag.

Example – Suppose you want to click on the first link. You can use below code.

```
element =
driver.find_element(:tag_name, 'A')
element.click
```

3.7 Link Text

This method can be used to identify only links in the web page.

Example – Suppose you want to click on the link 'Buy Selenium books'. You can use below syntax to click on the link.

```
element =
driver.find_element(:link_text,
'Buy Selenium books')

element.click
```

3.8 Partial Link Text

This method can be used to identify only links in the web page. Example – Suppose you want to click on the link which contains the word books. You can use below code.

```
element =
driver.find_element(:partial_link_t
ext, 'Buy')

element.click
```

4. Performing User Actions in Selenium

In this chapter, you will learn how to enter the data in webpage controls like editbox, combo box and how to select controls like checkbox, radio button. You will also know how to click on links, buttons or any other web element using selenium webdriver in Ruby.

Performing user actions involves identification of the elements on the webpage and then doing some operation like clicking on the button, entering the data in the editboxes, selecting a value from the drop down. Selenium Webdriver API in Ruby provides 3 important methods to enter data in web application.

1. send_keys
2. click
3. select_by

4.1 Entering data in Editboxes

We can enter the data in the editboxes using sendkeys method as illustrated in the below example.

Below selenium code will try to enter **Ruby** in the text box having name = **q**.

```
require "selenium-webdriver"

begin

driver = Selenium::WebDriver.for
:chrome
```

```
driver.navigate.to
"http://selenium-interview-
questions.blogspot.in/2014/03/selen
ium-webdriver-test-page.html"

#find the element using name
element =
driver.find_element(:name, 'q')

#enter data in the editbox - q

element.send_keys "Ruby"

#handle the exceptions if any
rescue Exception => e
  puts e.message
  puts e.backtrace.inspect
end

temp = gets.chomp

#close the browser

driver.quit
```

4.2 Selecting a value from the Combo boxes.

We can use the class -
Selenium::WebDriver::Support::Select while working with drop downs in Ruby. We can select the value from the dropdown using 3 different methods.

1. **text** – using the actual text displayed in drop down.

2. **value** –using the value of the option
3. **index** – using position of the item

Below example demonstrates how we can select the value from the drop down using text method.

Below code will first find out the drop down with name as city and then select the option from the drop down list with text as Pune.

```
option =
Selenium::WebDriver::Support::Selec
t.new(driver.find_element(:name,'ci
ty'))

option.select_by(:text,  "Pune")
```

Below example demonstrates how we can select the value from the drop down using value method.

Below code will first find out the drop down with name as **city** and then select the option from the drop down list with value as **Pune**.

```
option =
Selenium::WebDriver::Support::Selec
t.new(driver.find_element(:name,'ci
ty'))

option.select_by(:value,  "Pune")
```

Below example demonstrates how we can select the value from the drop down using index method. Below code will first find out the drop down with name as **city** and then select the option from the drop down list with index as **2**.

```
option =
Selenium::WebDriver::Support::Selec
t.new(driver.find_element(:name,'ci
ty'))

option.select_by(:index, 2)
```

Select class provides below methods.

1. deselect_all - Deselect all selected options.
2. deselect_by(how, what) - Deselect options by visible text, index or value.
3. first_selected_option - Get the first selected option in this select element.
4. multiple? - Does this select element support selecting multiple options?.
5. Options - Get all options for this select element.
6. select_all - Select all unselected options.
7. select_by(how, what) - Select options by visible text, index or value.
8. selected_options - Get all selected options for this select element.

You can find more information about the Select class at http://selenium.googlecode.com/svn-history/r15117/trunk/docs/api/rb/Selenium/WebDriver/Support/Select.html#select_by-instance_method

4.3 Clicking on buttons and links

We can click on the buttons and links using click method as illustrated in the below example. To identify the button or links, you can use identification methods like id, name, css, xpath etc.

Example – Suppose you want to click on the button with name "register". You can use below syntax to click on the button.

```
element =
driver.find_element(:name,
'register')

element.click
```

Example – Suppose you want to click on the link 'Buy Selenium books'. You can use below syntax to click on the link.

```
element =
driver.find_element(:link_text,
'Buy Selenium books')
```

```
element.click
```

4.4 Manipulating checkboxes and Radio Buttons

We can first see if the checkbox is selected using selected?
method. Then using click method we can perform the
operations such as selecting or deselecting the checkboxes
as illustrated in the below example.

```ruby
require "selenium-webdriver"

begin

driver = Selenium::WebDriver.for
:chrome
driver.navigate.to
"http://selenium-interview-
questions.blogspot.in/2014/03/selen
ium-webdriver-test-page.html"


element = driver.find_element(:css,
'input[value="hindi"]')

#if the element is selected, below
statement will print true

puts element.selected?

if element.selected? == false
```

```ruby
#select the checkbox if it is
unselected.
element.click
end

puts element.selected?

#print the title of the web page
currently open

puts driver.title

rescue Exception => e
  puts e.message
  puts e.backtrace.inspect
end

temp = gets.chomp

driver.quit
```

Similarly we can select or deselect the radio buttons as well.

5. Reading data from webpage in Selenium

In this chapter, you will learn how to read the data from webpage controls like editboxes, comboboxes etc. You will also learn how to see if the elements are enabled, disabled and selected. You will also know how to read the data from table on webpage using selenium webdriver.

Selenium API provides 2 important methods to read data from web elements.

1. **style** – gets the value of css property of the element
2. **attribute** – gets the value of given attribute.
3. **text** – gets the innertext of the element.

We can also check if

1. Element is displayed using **displayed?** method
2. Element is selected using **selected?** method
3. Element is enabled using **enabled?** Method

```ruby
require "selenium-webdriver"

begin

driver = Selenium::WebDriver.for
:chrome
```

```
driver.navigate.to
"http://selenium-interview-
questions.blogspot.in/2014/03/sel
enium-webdriver-test-page.html"
#attribute
element =
driver.find_element(:css,
'input[value="hindi"]')

#Print the value attribute's data

puts "Checkbox's value attribute
is  #{element.attribute('value')}
"
#below statement will print true
if the checkbox is selected
puts "Checkbox is selected
#{element.selected?} "

#below statement will print true
if the checkbox is enabled.

puts "Checkbox is enabled
#{element.enabled?} "

#below statement will print true
if the checkbox is displayed.


puts "Checkbox is displayed
#{element.displayed?} "

#style
```

```
element =
driver.find_element(:id,
'empdata')

puts "Table's border style ->
#{element.style('border')} "

#text
element =
driver.find_element(:tag_name,
'td')

puts "Data in first td tag is
#{element.text}"

rescue Exception => e
  puts e.message
  puts e.backtrace.inspect
end

temp = gets.chomp

driver.quit
```

5.1 Reading data from Editboxes and Combo boxes

We can get the data from editbox using attribute method.

In below code, we have entered a value – "ruby" in the editbox with name – **q** Then using attribute method, we have read the value entered in the same editbox.

```ruby
require "selenium-webdriver"

begin
driver = Selenium::WebDriver.for
:chrome
driver.navigate.to
"http://selenium-interview-
questions.blogspot.in/2014/03/selen
ium-webdriver-test-page.html"

#text
element =
driver.find_element(:name, 'q')
element.send_keys ("ruby")

puts "editbox value is
#{element.attribute('value')}"

rescue Exception => e
  puts e.message
  puts e.backtrace.inspect
end

temp = gets.chomp

driver.quit
```

Similarly we can read data from the drop down.

Below code snippet shows how we can read the value of selected option in combo box.

```
dropdown =
Selenium::WebDriver::Support::Selec
t.new(driver.find_element(:name,'ci
ty'))

#below statement will select the
value Pune from the dropdown.

dropdown.select_by(:text, "Pune")

#Print the selected option's value
puts
dropdown.first_selected_option.attr
ibute('value')
```

5.2 Reading data from checkboxes and Radio buttons

We can see if the checkbox is selected or not using selected? as illustrated in the below example.

5.3 Working with Tables in SELENIUM

Reading the data from the table is very easy in selenium webdriver.

We can identify the table using name, Id or xpath and then we can access the rows one by one using find_elements method.

For example – In below statement will find all row elements from the given table. Please note that t stands for the table object you have found using find_element method.

```
table = driver.find_element(:css,
'#empdata')

tr_element =
table.find_elements(:tag_name,
'tr')
```

Some common operations that we need to perform on the table are given below.

1. Get the Column Number for given column header.
2. Verify that data in the cell is correct as expected in the test step.
3. Difference between find_element and find_elements

Getting column number for the given column header. Consider below table having 4 columns. Suppose we want to find the position of the column Country.

EMP ID	EMP Name	Country	Operation
22	Obama	USA	Edit
31	Putin	Russia	Edit

Here is the code which will find the column number/position of Country.

44

```ruby
require "selenium-webdriver"

begin

driver = Selenium::WebDriver.for
:chrome
driver.navigate.to
"http://selenium-interview-
questions.blogspot.in/2014/03/selen
ium-webdriver-test-page.html"

table = driver.find_element(:id,
'empdata')

#get the collection of th tags from
the table

thtags=table.find_elements(:tag_nam
e,'th')

i=1
thtags.each do |th|
#break from the loop if the header
is Country

    if th.text.strip=="Country"
        break
    end
i = i + 1
```

```
end

#print the position of column
country
puts i

rescue Exception => e
  puts e.message
  puts e.backtrace.inspect
end

temp = gets.chomp

driver.quit
```

Verifying the data in the table cells.

Suppose that you want to verify that the country should be Russia for the employee with Id 31.

Below code will do it for you.

```
require "selenium-webdriver"
begin
driver = Selenium::WebDriver.for
:chrome
driver.navigate.to
"http://selenium-interview-
questions.blogspot.in/2014/03/selen
ium-webdriver-test-page.html"
```

```ruby
table = driver.find_element(:id,
'empdata')

#get the td with text 31
td=table.find_element(:xpath, '//td[
text()="31"]')

puts td.text

#get the second td element from
current td.
result =
td.find_element(:xpath, "./following
-sibling::td[2]").text

#result =
driver.execute_script('return
arguments[0].nextSibling.nextSiblin
g.innerText',td)

if result.strip=="Russia"
puts "Country is Russia....Test
passed."
else
puts "Country is not Russia....Test
failed."
end

rescue Exception => e
  puts e.message
  puts e.backtrace.inspect
end

temp = gets.chomp
```

```
driver.quit
```

Now let me explain the difference between find_element and find_elements.

Well – both the methods can be used to identify the elements from the webpage. The difference is that find_element returns only single matching element while find_elements returns all matching web elements from the webpage.

find_element Example

Consider below table having 4 columns. Suppose we want to print the EMP ID of the first record.

EMP ID	EMP Name	Country	Operation
22	Obama	USA	Edit
31	Putin	Russia	Edit

The html source code of the above table is given in below screenshot.

```
▼ <table id="empdata" style="border: solid 1px green;">
  ▼ <tbody>
    ▼ <tr>
        <th>EMP ID      </th>
        <th> EMP Name          
         </th>
        <th>Country         </th>
        <th>Operation </th>
      </tr>
    ▼ <tr>
        <td>22</td>
        <td>Obama</td>
        <td>USA</td>
      ▶ <td>…</td>
      </tr>
    ▶ <tr>…</tr>
    </tbody>
```

In below example, find_element method returns the first element with tag – td inside the html table with id empdata and prints the innertext.

```ruby
require "selenium-webdriver"
begin
driver = Selenium::WebDriver.for
:chrome
driver.navigate.to
"http://selenium-interview-
questions.blogspot.in/2014/03/selen
ium-webdriver-test-page.html"

element = driver.find_element(:id,
'empdata')

puts
element.find_element(:tag_name,'td'
).text
```

```
#element.send_keys "Ruby"

puts driver.title

rescue Exception => e
  puts e.message
  puts e.backtrace.inspect
end

temp = gets.chomp

driver.quit
```

find_elements Example
In below example, find_elements method returns the collection of all elements with tag – td and prints the innertext of each one. Please note how we have used List of webelements to store all elements returned by find_elements method.

```
require "selenium-webdriver"
begin
driver = Selenium::WebDriver.for
:chrome
driver.navigate.to
"http://selenium-interview-
questions.blogspot.in/2014/03/selen
ium-webdriver-test-page.html"

element = driver.find_element(:id,
'empdata')
```

```ruby
tdtags=element.find_elements(:tag_n
ame,'td')

tdtags.each do |td|
      puts td.text
end


#element.send_keys "Ruby"

puts driver.title

rescue Exception => e
  puts e.message
  puts e.backtrace.inspect
end

temp = gets.chomp

driver.quit
```

```
22
Obama
USA

31
Putin
Russia

Selenium Webdriver: Selenium Webdriver Test Page
```

6. Practical challenges and Solutions in SELENIUM

In this chapter, you will learn about various challenges that automation test engineers face while developing the automation scripts to test the web application. We will see different solutions that can be used to handle complex scenarios. We will also see how to add synchronization points in your selenium program using various methods.

Some of the challenges in selenium automations are given below.

1. Identifying elements relative to other elements.
2. Complex list boxes.
3. Event based code not getting invoked.
4. Handling dynamic html controls coming through Ajax request.

We can handle the challenges mentioned above by using any of the solutions mentioned below.

1. Using Advanced Xpath
2. Using DOM Methods in JavaScript
3. Using Synchronization methods

6.1 Using xpath to find out relative elements.

Let us try to understand the problem of relative elements.

Please have a look at below image.

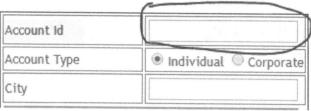

```
▼<table id="complexform" style="border: solid 1px blue;">
  ▼<tbody>
    ▼<tr>
        <td style="border: solid 1px red;">Account Id  
                       </td>
      ▼<td style="border: solid 1px red;">
          <input type="text" value>
        </td>
      </tr>
    ▶<tr>…</tr>
    ▶<tr>…</tr>
    ▶<tr>…</tr>
    </tbody>
  </table>
```

When I inspected the text box in chrome next to Account ID, I found the html code as shown below.

<input type="text" value>

Now as you can see this input element does not have any attribute that can be used to identify the element uniquely.

To solve this problem, we can have multiple solutions.

You can also inspect the above element at the url

53

http://selenium-interview-
questions.blogspot.in/2014/03/selenium-webdriver-test-
page.html using chrome.

To view the console, you can click on the button that is highlighted and encircled in below image.

You should see below screen after you click on above button.

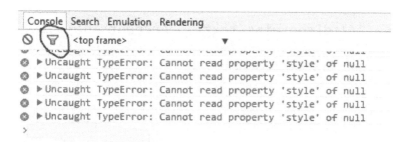

Console window in above image is showing JavaScript errors that is running behind the webpage. To hide these errors, click on the filter button that is encircled. You will see below options. Just click on warnings label. This will hide the error messages that you were seeing before.

Now you can test any kind of xpath and CSS expressions in the console.

```
⊘   ▽   <top frame>                    ▼
 Filter          Regex  All  Errors  Warnings  Info  Logs  Debug
 >  $x("//td[contains(text(),'City')]")
 <  [<td>City </td>, <td style="border: solid 1px red;">City</td>]
 >  $x("//td[contains(text(),'Account')]")
 <  [<td style="border: solid 1px red;">Account Id        
    <td style="border: solid 1px red;">Account Type</td>]
 > |
```

Coming back to the Account ID text box issue, we need to write such a xpath expression that will identify the textbox and xpath has to be strong as well so that in next release of the web application, it should work fine even if there is a change in the html of the web page.

Type below command in console window.

$x("//td[contains(text(),'Account Id')]")

You should see below output.

```
 ›  $x("//td[contains(text(),'Account Id')]")
 .  [<td style="border: solid 1px red;">Account Id  
 ›
```

So we have been able to find the td element which contains **Account ID** label. Please note that this is very strong xpath expression which can be used in multiple scenarios to identify the controls using the labels.

Even if the table cell has blank spaces or other tags like span or div, above xpath works well.

Now next step is to find the textbox which is located just next to it. Now type below command in the console and you should see that it identifies the desired textbox.

$x("//td[contains(text(),'Account Id')]/following-sibling::td/input")

We may use below xpath as well.

$x("//td[contains(text(),'Account Id')]/following-sibling::td[1]/input")

```
> $x("//td[contains(text(),'Account Id')]/following-sibling::td/input")
< [<input type="text" value>]
>
```

Let me explain what we have done here. Following-sibling is the keyword that can be used to identify the siblings of the current element.

Here we wanted to find the td element which is the sibling of the td containing **Account ID** text. We wanted to find the first sibling that's why we used above xpath. If we wanted second sibling, we would have used below xpath.

$x("//td[contains(text(),'Account Id')]/following-sibling::td[2]/input")

Once we have this xpath with us, we can easily identify the textbox using find element method.

This is a very strong xpath expression because it identifies the textbox in relation with the label. The automation code will not break in below scenarios.

1. If the account id textbox is moved to different row by the developer, it will not impact our automation code as long as label is associated with the textbox.

2. If developer adds some extra spaces or html tags like span, div inside the table cell, it will not impact our automation code.

Below table shows some of xpath expressions which can be very useful while trying to find the relative elements.

Find all tr tags that are ancestor of current td tag	//td/ancestor::tr
Find all tr tags that are descendant of current td tag	//td/descendant::tr
Find all following siblings of td	//td/following-sibling::td
Find all preceding siblings of td	//td/preceding-sibling::td
Find all the children of div	//div[text()='abc']/child::*
Find the parent of div	//div[text()='abc']/parent::*

So far we have been talking about xpath expressions to find the adjacent elements. In next topic let us try to solve the problem using JavaScript.

6.2 Using JavaScript HTML DOM to find out relative elements.

JavaScript provides below methods which can be used to find the elements relative to each other.

1. nextSibling – finds next sibling node
2. nextElementSibling – finds next sibling element
3. previousElementSibling – finds previous sibling element
4. previousSibling – finds previous sibling node
5. getElementsByTagName – returns collection of all elements with given tag say TD
6. attributes – gets collection of all attributes for given node.
7. childNodes – gets all child nodes
8. children – gets immediate child nodes
9. childElementCount – gets the count of children elements
10. getAttribute – gets the value for the given attribute.
11. firstChild – gets the first child node for current node.
12. firstElementChild – gets the first child element for the current node.
13. Focus – puts focus on the given element.
14. innerHTML – gets the html of given element.
15. innerText – gets the inner text of the element.
16. lastChild – gets the last child node of the given element.
17. lastElementChild – gets the last child element for the given node.

18. nodeName – gets the name for current node
19. nodeType – gets the type of the node
20. nodeValue – gets the value of the node
21. parentElement – gets the parent element for the node.
22. parentNode – gets the parent node of the given node.

Please note that all methods and properties mentioned in above list will not work on all browsers especially IE. So You will have to do some research to find out the alternative ways to perform specific operation.

Let us say we have got the reference of the td containing label Account Id in a variable say x.

Now we can get the next td element using below code in JavaScript.

Y = x.nextSibling

To get the textbox, we can use below code.

Textbox = x.nextSibling.getElementsByTagName("input")[0]

```
> y = $x("//td[contains(text(),'Account Id')]/following-sibling::td[1]")[0]
<  ▶<td style="border: solid 1px red;">…</td>
> y.getElementsByTagName("input")[0]
<  <input type="text" value>
```

Here is working code.

```
require "selenium-webdriver"
```

```ruby
begin
driver = Selenium::WebDriver.for
:chrome

driver.navigate.to
"http://selenium-interview-
questions.blogspot.in/2014/03/selen
ium-webdriver-test-page.html"

table = driver.find_element(:id,
'complexform')

td = driver.find_element(:xpath,
'//td[contains(text(),"Account
Id")]')

#pass the td element to execute
script method
text =
driver.execute_script("return
arguments[0].nextSibling.getElement
sByTagName('input')[0]",td)

#enter the value 89879 in below
editbox.
text.send_keys "89879"

rescue Exception => e
  puts e.message
  puts e.backtrace.inspect
end

temp = gets.chomp
```

```
driver.quit
```

Similarly We can find the elements that are located previous to the current element using previousSibling property.

6.3 Handling Complex Web lists

Consider below screenshot. This is a flight booking page. You can select the source city using From drop down box.

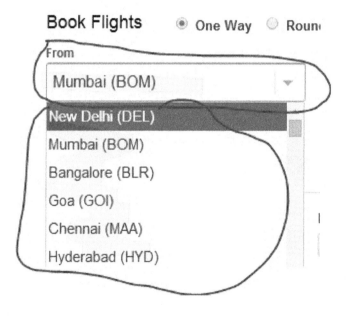

But if you inspect the elements, you will find that this is **not a standard combo box – select HTML element**.

Instead it is actually a combination of 2 Elements.

Input Element with id as **in_gi_source**

Div Element with class as **Suggest_combo_input i_custom**

```
▼<div class="Suggest_combo_box h_width">
  ►<input autocomplete="off" type="text" class=
  "Suggest_combo_input i_custom" id="in_gi_source" tabindex="3">
    <input type="hidden" name="gi_source" id="gi_source" value=
    "DEL">
    <input type="hidden" name="gi_source_new_value" value=
    "false">
```

```
</div>
▼<div class="Suggest_combo_list e_pos" style="display: block;
left: 0px; max-height: 233px; min-height: 30px; height: auto;">
    <div class="en_custom          " style="width: 100%; overflow
    hidden;">New Delhi (DEL)</div>
    <div class="en_custom          " style="width: 100%;
    overflow: hidden;">Mumbai (BOM)</div>
    <div class="en_custom          " style="width: 100%; overflow
    hidden;">Bangalore (BLR)</div>
    <div class="en_custom    Suggest_selected_option" style=
    "width: 100%; overflow: hidden;">Goa (GOI)</div>
    <div class="en_custom " style="width: 100%; overflow:
    hidden;">Chennai (MAA)</div>
    <div class="en_custom " style="width: 100%; overflow:
    hidden;">Hyderabad (HYD)</div>
    <div class="en_custom " style="width: 100%; overflow:
    hidden;">Kolkata (CCU)</div>
    <div class="en_custom" style="width: 100%; overflow:
```

So selecting a value from such drop down will not be so simple. We can not use **Select** class and its methods (select by text, index, value) to select the option from the drop down.

You will have to follow below steps to select the option from the dropdown.

Suppose you want to select **Chennai** option. Then you will have to first find the div with class **Suggest_combo_input i_custom.**

Then you will have to find the div containing **Chennai** as text.

Then enter that value in the Input Element with id as **in_gi_source**

We can write the xpath for this requirement as below.

//div[@class='Suggest_combo_list e_pos']

But this xpath returns 2 **div** elements.

```
>  $x("//div[@class='Suggest_combo_list e_pos']")
⟨  [▶<div class="Suggest_combo_list e_pos" style="display: block; left: 0p
    ▶<div class="Suggest_combo_list e_pos" style="display: none;">…</div>]
>  $x("(//div[@class='Suggest_combo_list e_pos'])[1]")
⟨  [▶<div class="Suggest_combo_list e_pos" style="display: block; left: 0p
>  |
```

To get the first div, we will have to reframe the xpath expression.

(//div[@class='Suggest_combo_list e_pos'])[1]

Then we need to find the div tag containing text Chennai.

Xpath will be

(//div[@class='Suggest_combo_list e_pos'])[1]/div[contains(text(),'Chennai')]

```
> $x("(//div[@class='Suggest_combo_list e_pos'])[1]/div[contains(text(),'Chennai')]")
< [<div class="en_custom " style="width: 100%; overflow: hidden;">Chennai (MAA)</div>]
> |
```

Once we get this element, we can easily read text inside it and set that value in input element using Send Keys method. But send keys may not work in this case. So you can use Java script to set the value of input box using below code.

x.value = "Chennai (MAA)"

```
> $$("#in_gi_source")[0].value="Chennai (MAA)"
< "Chennai (MAA)"
. |
```

6.4 Events not getting triggered.

The way in which we have selected the value from the combo box in previous section may or may not work if developer has written some JavaScript code on click event of the option. JavaScript code will not get invoked in such scenario.

 So basically when we select the value from the web combo box (dropdown), HTML DOM of the webpage changes. It may change the visibility of the some of the controls like edit boxes or drop downs. It may do some ajax calls to the server by using JavaScript code.

So basically when we do some operation on the web elements , specific event handlers (java script code or function) get called. But performing the same operation with selenium API may not call these event handlers.

To handle such situation, we will have to simulate the actual user behaviour clicking on the option in the drop down.

So you will have to again find the option item using same xpath.

(//div[@class='Suggest_combo_list e_pos'])[1]/div[contains(text(),'Chennai')]

Then use click method.

If you are still not able to invoke the JavaScript code, you can try below code.

```
var evt =
document.createEvent("HTMLEvents")

//Set the event type like change,
click, mouseup, mousedown

evt.initEvent "change", true, true

//Dispatch the event on desired
object.

x.dispatchEvent(evt)

//here x is the element on which we
want to fire the event.
```

Please note that above code is written in JavaScript. You can execute above code using execute_script method.

6.5 Ajax and Synchronization

We can set the implicit timeout using below code

driver.manage.timeouts.implicit_wait = 20

This means that selenium script will wait for maximum 20 seconds for element to exist. If Web element does not exist within 20 seconds, it will throw an exception.

This will be applicable to all elements on the webpage.

Now we are going to have a look at explicit synchronization method. We can insert explicit synchronization points in the script using Wait class.

wait for a specific element to show up

```
wait =
Selenium::WebDriver::Wait.new(:time
out => 10)

wait.until {
driver.find_element(:id =>
"empdata") }
```

This code is useful when dynamic html loads in the page asynchronously using Ajax. We can wait for specific element until it gets displayed.

7. Advanced Operations in Selenium

In this chapter, you will learn how to perform various mouse and keyboard operations like double click, right click, drag and drop etc. You will also learn how to take screenshot, how to execute JavaScript from selenium webdriver and how to upload a file in selenium.

7.1 Mouse and keyboard Events in SELENIUM

With Selenium webdriver's Actions class, we can perform all kinds of complex keyboard and mouse operations.

We can perform operations as mentioned below.

1. Click
2. click_and_hold
3. context_click
4. double_click
5. drag_and_drop
6. drag_and_drop_by
7. key_down
8. key_up
9. move_by
10. move_to
11. release
12. send_keys

Examples -

<u>Below code will right click on the given element.</u>

```
driver.action.context_click(table).
perform
```

Below code shows how we can drag and drop elements using selenium webdriver in Ruby. Below code will drag element1 and drop it to element2.

```
driver.action.drag_and_drop(elemen
t1, element2).perform
```

You can send keys using below codes.

```
:null,   :cancel, :help, :backspace,
:tab, :clear , :return, :enter,
:shift,    :left_shift,  :control,
:left_control, :alt
:left_alt, :pause, :escape, :space,
:page_up, :page_down
:end, :home, :left, :arrow_left,
:up, :arrow_up, :right,
:arrow_right, :down, :arrow_down,
:insert, :delete, :semicolon,
:equals, :numpad0, :numpad1,
:numpad2, :numpad3, :numpad4,
:numpad5, :numpad6, :numpad7,
:numpad8, :numpad9, :multiply,
:add, :separator, :subtract
:decimal, :divide, :f1, :f2, :f3,
:f4, :f5, :f6, :f7, :f8, :f9, :f10,
:f11, :f12, :meta, :command
```

For example – Suppose you want to send tab key, then below code will do it.

```
element.send_keys :tab
```

To send the combination of key like ctrl + C, use below code

```
element.send_keys [:control, 'c']
```

To select an option from the context menu you may try below code.

```
driver.action.context_click(table).
send_keys(:arrow_down).send_keys(:a
rrow_down).send_keys(:return).perfo
rm
```

```
driver.action.context_click(table).
perform
sleep(2)
driver.find_element(:link_text,
'Reload').click
```

7.2 Taking Screen shots in SELENIUM

Below code will illustrate how we can take screen shots in selenium in Ruby.

```ruby
require 'rubygems'

require "selenium-webdriver"

begin
driver = Selenium::WebDriver.for
:chrome

driver.navigate.to
"http://selenium-interview-
questions.blogspot.in/2014/03/selen
ium-webdriver-test-page.html"

table = driver.find_element(:id,
'empdata')

#take the screenshot and save the
file in png format.
driver.save_screenshot("myscreensho
t.png")

rescue Exception => e
  puts e.message
  puts e.backtrace.inspect
end

temp = gets.chomp

driver.quit
```

7.3 Executing JavaScript in SELENIUM

We can use execute_script method of driver to execute JavaScript in Selenium.

Below code will illustrate how we can execute JavaScript in selenium in Ruby.

```ruby
require "selenium-webdriver"

begin

driver = Selenium::WebDriver.for
:chrome

driver.navigate.to
"http://selenium-interview-
questions.blogspot.in/2014/03/selen
ium-webdriver-test-page.html"

table = driver.find_element(:id,
'empdata')

#print all data from the current
page

puts driver.execute_script("return
document.body.innerText")

#print the data from table element
```

```ruby
puts driver.execute_script("return
arguments[0].innerText",table)

rescue Exception => e
  puts e.message
  puts e.backtrace.inspect
end

temp = gets.chomp

driver.quit
```

Note - In above code, we have passed the web element table as an argument to execute_script method.

7.4 uploading files in SELENIUM

Uploading file using selenium webdriver is very simple. All you have to do is – find the input element having type attribute's value as **file** and then use send_keys to send the path of the file we want to upload.

Below code will illustrate how we can upload a file using selenium webdriver in Ruby.

```ruby
require "selenium-webdriver"

begin
```

```ruby
driver = Selenium::WebDriver.for
:chrome
driver.navigate.to
"http://selenium-interview-
questions.blogspot.in/2014/03/selen
ium-webdriver-test-page.html"

myfile= driver.find_element(:xpath,
'//input[@type="file"]')

myfile.send_keys "c:\\abc.xls"
driver.find_element(:xpath,
'//input[@name="register"]').click

rescue Exception => e
  puts e.message
  puts e.backtrace.inspect
end

temp = gets.chomp

driver.quit
```

8. Working with frames and Windows in SELENIUM

> *In this chapter, you will learn how to work with multiple frames, windows and alerts in selenium webdriver in Ruby.*

All web applications involve the frames, alerts and window. Selenium webdriver provides the way to handle with alerts, frames and windows using switch_to method

8.1 Handling Frames

To work with frames we need to switch to the frame and then perform the operation inside it.

You can identify the frame in web page using 3 ways.

1. By Name
2. By Index
3. By Using any of the element identification methods.

For example – If you want to switch to the frame with name **fb,** you can use below code.

```
driver.switch_to.frame "fb"
```

You can also use the **index** to identify the frame in browser window.

For example- If you want to switch to the frame at position number 1, you can use below code.

```
driver.switch_to.frame 1
```

If you may also identify the frame using any of the element identification methods. Suppose if you want to switch to the frame with id xyz, you can switch to that frame using below code.

```
driver.switch_to.frame
driver.find_element(:id, 'xyz')
```

Here is the complete script to identify the frame with name - **g**

```
require "selenium-webdriver"

begin

driver = Selenium::WebDriver.for
:chrome

driver.navigate.to
"http://selenium-interview-
questions.blogspot.in/2014/03/selen
ium-webdriver-test-page.html"
```

```
driver.manage.window.maximize

#driver.switch_to.frame "g"
driver.switch_to.frame
driver.find_element(:xpath,
'//iframe[@name="g"]')

driver.find_element(:link_text,
'Software Tutorials').click

driver.switch_to.default_content

rescue Exception => e
  puts e.message
  puts e.backtrace.inspect
end

temp = gets.chomp

driver.quit
```

8.2 Working with Alerts

We can handle alerts using Alert Interface in Ruby Web Driver. At first, we need to get the alert reference using below syntax.

```
Alert = driver.switch_to.alert
```

Then we can click on Ok button using below syntax.

```
Alert .accept
```

Then we can click on Cancel button using below syntax.

```
Alert.dismiss
```

To get the text displayed in the alert, you can use text method.

```
puts Alert.text
```

Here is the working example showing how we can handle the alerts in Selenium-Ruby.

```
require "selenium-webdriver"

begin

driver = Selenium::WebDriver.for
:chrome

driver.navigate.to
"http://selenium-interview-
questions.blogspot.in/2014/03/selen
ium-webdriver-test-page.html"
driver.manage.window.maximize
```

```
driver.find_element(:xpath,
'//input[@name="register"]').click

Alert = driver.switch_to.alert

#print the text displayed on alert
puts Alert.text

#click on Ok button on alert.
Alert.accept

rescue Exception => e
  puts e.message
  puts e.backtrace.inspect
end

temp = gets.chomp

driver.quit
```

8.3 Working with multiple browser Windows

Below code will show you how we can handle multiple browser windows in selenium in Ruby.

There are 2 methods which can be used to find out the handles of the windows.

1. window_handle
2. window_handles

window_handle method returns the handle of the current browser window.

window_handles method returns the handles of the browser windows opened by selenium ruby script.

We can switch to any of the window using this handle as shown in below code.

```
driver.switch_to.window anyhandle
```

```ruby
require "selenium-webdriver"
begin

driver = Selenium::WebDriver.for
:chrome

driver.navigate.to http://selenium-
interview-
questions.blogspot.in/2014/03/selen
ium-webdriver-test-page.html

driver.manage.window.maximize

driver.find_element(:link_text,
'Buy Selenium books').click

#print the handle of current
browser window
puts driver.window_handle
```

```ruby
#get the handles of all browser
windows opened by driver.
windowhandles =
driver.window_handles

puts "Total Window Handles
#{windowhandles.length}"

puts windowhandles[0]

puts windowhandles[1]

driver.switch_to.window
windowhandles[1]
sleep(4)

puts driver.title

rescue Exception => e
  puts e.message
  puts e.backtrace.inspect
end

temp = gets.chomp

driver.quit
```

9. Important Built-in Function in Ruby.

In this chapter, you will learn important built in classes and their methods in Ruby to work with strings, files, date and time, Math etc. You will need these methods when doing validations and comparisons while doing functional testing of web applications.

9.1 Working with Strings in Ruby

We must know below string operations while working with selenium.

```ruby
require "selenium-webdriver"
begin

str = "Selenium in Ruby"

#Capitalize the string
puts "String in capitalized form
#{str.capitalize}"

#Convert the string to lower case
puts "String in lower case
#{str.downcase}"

#Convert the string to upper case
```

```ruby
puts "String in upper case
#{str.upcase}"

#Remove the leading spaces from the
string
puts "String after removing leading
spaces #{str.lstrip}"

#Remove the trailing spaces from
the string
puts "String after removing
trailing spaces #{str.rstrip}"

#Remove the leading and trailing
spaces from the string
puts "String after removing leading
and trailing spaces #{str.strip}"

#Find the length of the string
puts "String length is
#{str.length}"

#Find the substring
if str.include? "Ruby"
   puts "String includes Ruby"
else
   puts "String does not include
Ruby"
end

#replacing one occurrence of the
string
newstr = str.sub! 'Ruby', 'Java
Java'
```

```ruby
puts newstr

#replacing all occurances of the
string
newstr = str.gsub! 'Java', 'Ruby'
puts newstr


#getting substring from  the string
newstr = str[2,3]
puts "first 3 chars from the 2nd
position of the string"
puts newstr

#Splitting the string
newstr = str.split(' ')
puts "String after split"
puts newstr[0]
puts newstr[1]

rescue Exception => e
  puts e.message
  puts e.backtrace.inspect
end
temp = gets.chomp
driver.quit
```

9.2 Working with Date and Time

In all banking projects, you will have to calculate the date differences or find the future or past date. So you must know how to do this in Ruby.

```ruby
require "selenium-webdriver"
begin

#current time stamp
puts Time.now

time = Time.now

#print year
puts time.year

#print month
puts time.month

#print day
puts time.day

#format the date and time
puts time.strftime("%Y-%m-%d
%H:%M:%S")

#print the formatted date
puts time.strftime("%Y-%m-%d")

#print the time zone
puts time.zone

#print the week day number - sunday
means 0
```

```
puts time.wday

#add 1 day
puts time + 24 * 60 * 60

#subtract 1 day
puts time - 24 * 60 * 60


rescue Exception => e
  puts e.message
  puts e.backtrace.inspect
end

temp = gets.chomp

driver.quit
```

9.3 Working with Files and Folders

Below code will create new file at given path and append some data in it. If file already exists, it will be overwritten.

```
require "selenium-webdriver"
begin

path_to_file = 'f:\\sel-
ruby\\abc.txt'

myfile = File.new(path_to_file,
"a+")
```

```ruby
if myfile
    myfile.syswrite("This is written
to file")
   myfile.close
else
    puts "Unable to open file!"
end

puts File.read(path_to_file)

File.delete(path_to_file) if
File.exist?(path_to_file)

rescue Exception => e
   puts e.message
   puts e.backtrace.inspect
end

temp = gets.chomp

driver.quit
```

9.4 Maths

Important Maths related methods provided in Ruby are given below.

1. Round - rounds the number to specific number of decimals.
2. Pow - to find value of x^y.

```ruby
require "selenium-webdriver"
begin

#rounds the number to nearest
integer value
puts 3.893.round

#rounds the number upto 1 decimal
puts 3.893.round(1)


#rounds the number upto 2 decimal
puts 3.893.round(2)

#find the floor value for the
number
puts 1.677.floor

#find the ceil value for the number
puts 1.677.ceil

#find the value of x^y
puts 2**3

rescue Exception => e
  puts e.message
  puts e.backtrace.inspect
end

temp = gets.chomp

driver.quit
```

9.5 Using Ruby Arrays

Arrays are used to store the multiple elements of the same type in adjacent locations.

```ruby
name = ['sagar', 'amol', 'Obama', 'Putin',]
puts name[0]
puts name[1]
puts name[2]
puts name[3]

puts "\nloop to iterate through the name array\n"

name.each do |name|
  puts name
end

temp = gets.chomp
```

9.6 Find the execution time in Ruby.

When executing test cases using selenium webdriver, we need to find the execution time of test cases. Below example illustrates how we can find the execution time in Ruby.

Please note that we need to include **time** gem at the beginning of the program

```ruby
require 'time'
require "selenium-webdriver"
begin

#current time stamp
puts Time.now

time = Time.now

time1 = Time.parse("2014-08-05 19:10:10")

puts "difference between times in min is "

puts (time1-time)/60

rescue Exception => e
  puts e.message
  puts e.backtrace.inspect
end

temp = gets.chomp

driver.quit
```

10. Exception in Selenium Webdriver

In this chapter, you will learn how to handle exceptions that might occur while working with selenium webdriver in Ruby.

10.1 Exception handling in Ruby

Below example will illustrate how we can handle the exceptions in RUBY using begin … rescue blocks.

Please remember that we can have many catch blocks after try block. Whenever exception occurs, it is thrown and caught by the catch block. In catch block we can write the code for recovery.

10.2 Exceptions in Selenium Webdriver

Below is the list of most commonly occurring exceptions When working with selenium webdriver.

1. ElementNotVisibleError
2. InvalidElementStateError
3. InvalidSelectorError
4. NoAlertPresentError
5. NoSuchElementError
6. NoSuchFrameError
7. NoSuchWindowError
8. StaleElementReferenceError
9. UnhandledAlertError

Let us try to understand the meaning of each of these exceptions. We will also discuss about how to avoid these exceptions.

ElementNotVisibleError

This kind of exception occurs when the element you are trying to perform operation on is not visible. The style attribute – visibility of the element or it's parent is hidden. To avoid this kind of exception, ensure that element is visible.

InvalidElementStateError

This kind of exception occurs when the element you are trying to perform operation on is in invalid state. There are many scenarios when this exception might occur.
For example Trying to invoke **clear** method on link will trigger this exception.
To avoid this exception, make sure that you are performing the valid operation on correct element.

InvalidSelectorError

This kind of exception occurs when the xpath or css selector expression you are using to identify the element on the webpage is not correct by syntax.
For example – below statement will throw InvalidSelectorError

```
x = driver.find_element(:xpath,
"Images[:]")
```

NoAlertPresentError

This kind of exception occurs when you are trying to switch to the alert but that alert is not present on web page.
To avoid this error, ensure that alert is really present on the webpage before switching to it.

NoSuchElementError

This kind of exception occurs when the find_element method is not able to find the element by the given identification method.
 To avoid this exception make sure that css or xpath expression you are using is correct. Also ensure that you are on right page and element is really loaded in the webpage. Some elements take longer time to load. So try to add synchronization points before trying to find them.

NoSuchFrameError

This kind of exception occurs when the frame you are trying to switch to does not exist.
To avoid this exception make sure that css or xpath expression you are using is correct. Also ensure that you are on right page and frame is really loaded in the webpage.

NoSuchWindowError

This kind of exception occurs when the window you are trying to switch to does not exist.

To avoid this exception make sure that window you are trying to switch is really open and window handle you are using is also correct.

StaleElementReferenceError

This kind of exception occurs when the element you are trying to perform operation on is removed and re-added to the web page. This usually happens when Ajax changes your page source asynchronously. In other words, A StaleElementReferenceError is thrown when the element you were interacting is destroyed and then recreated using Ajax. When this happens the reference to the element in the DOM that you previously had becomes stale and you are no longer able to use this reference to interact with the element in the DOM. When this happens you will need to refresh your reference, or in real world terms find the element again.

To avoid this exception, try to find the element again and again until you do not get StaleElementReferenceError.

UnhandledAlertError

This kind of exception occurs when alert is present on the webpage and you are trying to perform some operation on other elements on the webpage. To avoid this error, ensure that you dismiss the alert and then execute the automation script.

11. Excel Programming in SELENIUM

In this chapter, you will learn how to read and write Microsoft excel files in Ruby.

11.1 Creating and writing data to Excel Workbook

When we design a test automation framework in Selenium, we usually store the test data inside excel sheets.

Below example demonstrates how we can create and write to excel workbook. Please note that below code will work only on windows based OS.

```ruby
# Require the WIN32OLE library
require 'win32ole'

begin
# Create an instance of the Excel
application object
xl =
WIN32OLE.new('Excel.Application')

# Make Excel visible
xl.Visible = true
```

```ruby
#Suppress the warnings
xl.displayAlerts = false

# Add a new Workbook object
wb = xl.Workbooks.Add

# Get the first Worksheet
ws = wb.Worksheets(1)

# Set the name of the worksheet tab
ws.Name = 'Selenium Training'

#write some data into worksheet
cell A1
ws.Cells(1,1).Value = "Selenium"

#write some data into worksheet
cell A2
ws.Cells(2,1).Value = "Ruby"

rescue Exception => e
  puts e.message
  puts e.backtrace.inspect
end

# Save the workbook
wb.SaveAs('f:\sel-
ruby\workbook.xls')

# Close the workbook
wb.Close

# Quit Excel
xl.Quit
```

11.2 Reading data from existing workbook

We can read the data from excel sheets using below code. Please note that we have used win32ole library to read and write the excel data. Those who are familiar with VBA coding will be able to understand the code very easily.

```ruby
# Require the WIN32OLE library
require 'win32ole'

begin
# Create an instance of the Excel
application object
xl =
WIN32OLE.new('Excel.Application')

# Make Excel visible
xl.Visible = true

#Suppress the warnings
xl.displayAlerts = false

# Add a new Workbook object
wb = xl.Workbooks.open('f:\sel-
ruby\workbook.xls')

# Get the first Worksheet
ws = wb.Worksheets(1)
```

```ruby
# Print the name of the worksheet
tab
puts ws.Name

#Read data from worksheet cell A1
puts ws.Cells(1,1).Value

#Read data into worksheet cell A2
puts ws.Cells(2,1).Value

rescue Exception => e
  puts e.message
  puts e.backtrace.inspect
end

# Close the workbook
 wb.Close

 # Quit Excel
 xl.Quit

 a = gets.chomp
```

12. Framework Designing in SELENIUM

In this chapter, you will learn about various automation testing frameworks in Selenium. You will also learn about how to design the keyword driven automation framework in Ruby.

There are 3 types of automation frameworks that can be designed in selenium. Please note that In any other automation tools like QTP, Win runner similar kinds of frameworks are popular.

12.1 Data Driven Framework

In data driven framework, importance is given to test data than multiple functionality of application. We design data driven framework to work with applications where we want to test same flow with different test data.

12.2 Hybrid Framework

This is the combination of keyword and data driven frameworks.

After analysing the application, you can decide what kind of framework best suits your needs and then you can design automation framework in SELENIUM.

12.3 Keyword Driven Framework

In Keyword Driven Framework , Importance is given to functions than Test Data. when we have to test multiple functionalities we can go for keyword frameworks. Each keyword is mapped to function in SELENIUM library and application.

Components of Keyword Driven framework

Keyword driven Automation Framework is most popular test automation framework. It is very easy to design and learn a keyword driven automation framework in SELENIUM.

In this article I will explain you all details about how we can design and use keyword driven automation framework in SELENIUM with example. I will also explain the advantages and disadvantages of keyword driven automation framework in SELENIUM.
In keyword driven automation framework, focus is mainly on keywords/functions and not the test data. This means we focus on creating the functions that are mapped to the functionality of the application.

For example - Suppose you have a flight reservation application which provides many features like

1. Login to the application

2. Search Flights

3. Book Flight tickets

4. Cancel Tickets

5. Fax Order

6. View Reports

To implement the keyword driven automation framework for this kind of application we will create functions in Ruby for each functionality mentioned above. We pass the test data and test object details to these functions.

The main components of keyword driven automation framework in SELENIUM

Each keyword driven automation framework has some common components as mentioned below.

1. Scripts Library

2. Test Data (generally in excel format)

3. SELENIUM - Settings and Environment Variables

4. Reports - (Generally in HTML format)

5. Test Driver Script Method

Test Data Sheet in keyword driven framework in SELENIUM.

Generally automated test cases are stored in excel sheets. From SELENIUM script ,we read excel file and then row by row we execute the functions in a test case. Each test case is implemented as a set of keywords.

Common columns in Data sheet are mentioned below.

1. Test case ID - Stores the Test Case ID mapped to Manual Test Cases.

2. Test Case Name - Name of the Test cases/ Scenario.

3. Execute Flag - if Marked Y -> Test case will be executed

4. Test_Step_Id - Steps in a test case

5. Keyword - Mapped to function in library file.

6. Object Types - Class of the object e.g. winedit, webedit, swfbutton etc

7. Object Names -Names of objects in OR .

8. Object Values - Actual test data to be entered in the objects.

9. Parameter1 - This is used to control the execution flow in the function.

Test_ID	TC_Name	Execute	Test_Step_ID	Keyword	Object_Types	Object_Names	Object_Values	Parameter1
1	Login To App	Y	Step1	login	winedit;winedit	userid;password	salunke;mercury	
			Step2	Insert_Order	wincombobox;wincombobo	flyfrom;flyto	london;paris	
			Step3	Fax_Order				Order_Id

Please note that this is just a sample data sheet that can be used in keyword driven framework. There could be customized data sheets for each project depending upon the requirement and design.

For example there could be more parameters or test data is stored in the databases.

Test Driver Script in SELENIUM.

This is the heart of keyword driven / data driven frameworks. This is the main script that interacts with all modules mentioned above.

Main tasks that are accomplished by driver script are ->

1. Read data from the Environment variables.

2. Call report module to create Report folders / files

3. Read Excel file

4. Call the function mapped to keyword.

5. Log the result

13. Miscellaneous topics on SELENIUM

> *In this chapter, you will get to know about selenium IDE, Selenium Grid and Junit. You will also learn about multi-browser testing, challenges and limitations of Selenium Webdriver.*

13.1 Selenium IDE.

Selenium IDE is a Firefox plugin which records and plays back user interactions with the browser. Use this to either create simple scripts or assist in exploratory testing. You can also export the test scripts in languages like Ruby, C#, Ruby and Python.

You can install Selenium IDE xpi file from
http://release.seleniumhq.org/selenium-ide/

Follow below steps to install Selenium IDE

1. Open Firefox browser
2. Go to tools -> Add-ons
3. Click on Gear icon ->Install add on from file
4. Browse xpi file downloaded from selenium site
5. Click on install now and restart Firefox

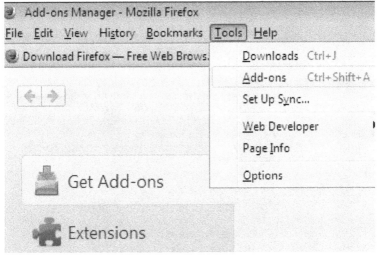

Figure 0-1 - Open Add-Ons page in Firefox

Click on the gear icon and then select Install Add-on From File...

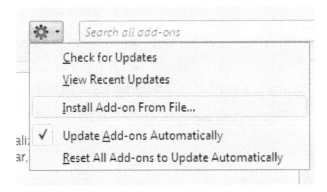

Figure 0-2 - Install Add-on from file

Then Browse to the selenium IDE xpi file downloaded from selenium website and select it. You will see next image.

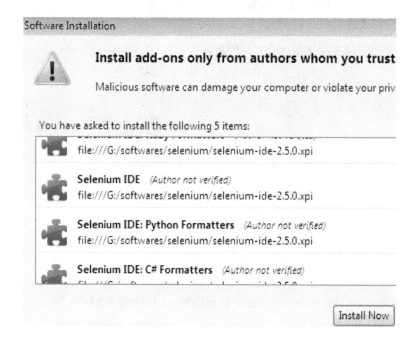

Figure 0-3 - Install Selenium IDE add on

After you click on Install Now button, Add-on will be installed and you will have to restart the Firefox. Then you will have to go to the Tools -> Selenium IDE to start it.

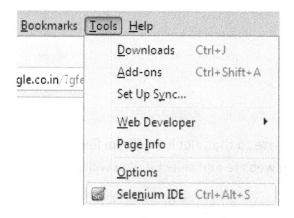

Figure 0-4 - Launch Selenium IDE in Firefox

105

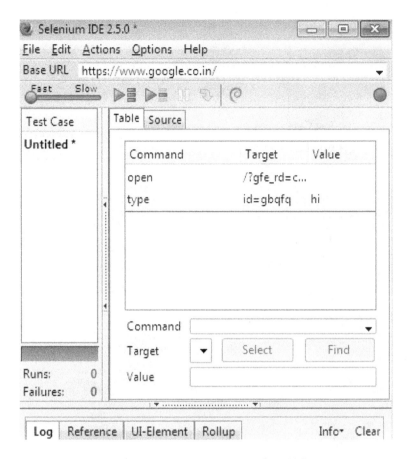

Figure 0-5 - Selenium IDE main Window

When you open selenium IDE, recording is automatically started. You can perform any operation on the web page open in Firefox browser. As you can see in previous figure, It shows the commands as we record it. We can export the test case in many languages as shown in next figure.

106

File Edit Actions Options Help

New Test Case	Ctrl+N	n/ ▼
Open...	Ctrl+O	⊘ ●
Save Test Case	Ctrl+S	
Save Test Case As...		
Export Test Case As...	▶	Ruby / RSpec / WebDriver
Recent Test Cases	▶	Ruby / Test::Unit / WebDriver
Add Test Case...	Ctrl+D	Ruby / RSpec / Remote Control
Properties...		Ruby / Test::Unit / Remote Con
		Python 2 / unittest / WebDriver
New Test Suite		Python 2 / unittest / Remote Co
Open Test Suite...		Java / JUnit 4 / WebDriver
Save Test Suite		Java / JUnit 4 / WebDriver Backe
Save Test Suite As...		Java / JUnit 4 / Remote Control
Export Test Suite As...	▶	Java / JUnit 3 / Remote Control
Recent Test Suites	▶	Java / TestNG / Remote Contro
Close (X)	Ctrl+W	C# / NUnit / WebDriver

Figure 0-6 - Export test case in various languages

13.2 Selenium Grid.

Selenium Grid is used for running tests in parallel on different machines(called as nodes) from central machine(called as Hub).

Hub acts as a central server. Based upon the configuration of the nodes (browser , OS), Hub will select the node and trigger the execution.

13.3 Multi-Browser Testing using Selenium.

Selenium webdriver is very popular tool to test cross-browser compatibility of the web applications.

The code you write for one browser say Firefox can be used as it is for other browsers like Internet Explorer, Chrome, Safari etc.

13.4 Limitations of Selenium Webdriver.

Below is the list of limitation of selenium.

1. Selenium webdriver only supports testing of web applications.

2. Desktop based applications developed in Ruby and .Net can not be automated using Selenium Webdriver

3. We can not automate or verify the Flash Content, Silverlight Apps , and Applet Contents using Selenium Webdriver.

www.ingramcontent.com/pod-product-compliance
Lightning Source LLC
Chambersburg PA
CBHW052149070326
40689CB00050B/2528